Logical Reasoning

Book 3

Mukhtar Ahemad.

MACAW BOOKS

www.macawbooks.com

shop online @
www.macawbooksonline.com

Published by Macaw Books

ISBN 978-1-60346-291-4
www.macawbooks.com

Printed in India

Contents

1 Guessing Numbers

Read the statement carefully and guess the number:

Example: A two-digit number which is greater than 20, less than 35 and has nine in ones' place.

a) 32
b) 29
c) 39
d) 25

Answer: The number is greater than 20 and less than 35. Therefore, the highest and lowest possible answers are 21, 22, 23, 24, 25, 26, 27, 28, 29, 30, 31, 32, 33, and 34. Since the unknown number has nine in ones' place, the correct option will be 29. Hence, the answer is: b) 29

1 A two-digit number which is greater than 55 and less than 61, and is a multiple of 5.

a) 56   b) 57   c) 59   d) 60

2 A two-digit number which is a multiple of 4, 6 and 8 and is less than 30.

a) 20   b) 22   c) 24   d) 26

3 A two-digit number which is greater than 86, less than 100 and has 4 in ones' place.

a) 94   b) 84   c) 92   d) 98

4 A two-digit number which is greater than 30, less than 35 and multiple of 4.

a) 31   b) 32   c) 33   d) 34

5 An even two-digit number which is greater than 96.

a) 98   b) 99   c) 97   d) 100

6 A two-digit number which is a multiple of 9 and 11.

a) 33   b) 66   c) 99   d) 11

7 A two-digit number which is greater than 90 and has 7 in ones' place.

    a)   87   b)   77   c)   107   d)   97

8 A two-digit number which is divisible by 7 and has 0 in ones' place.

    a)   21   b)   63   c)   35   d)   70

9 A two-digit number which is greater than 37, has 3 in tens' place and is divisible by 3.

    a)   38   b)   39   c)   36   d)   30

10 A two-digit number which is divisible by 5, have 6 in tens' place and is not a multiple of 10.

    a)   65   b)   75   c)   60   d)   70

Q2. **Guess the two numbers using the information disclosed below in each statement:**

Example: The sum of two numbers is 6 and difference is 0. Guess the two numbers.

a) 1 and 1
b) 2 and 2
c) 3 and 3
d) 4 and 3

Answer: The difference between the two numbers is 0; therefore, the two numbers must be same. The sum of the two numbers is 6; therefore, the two numbers cannot exceed 3. The possibilities are as follows:

Sum	Difference
1 + 1 = 2	1 − 1 = 0
2 + 2 = 4	2 − 2 = 0
3 + 3 = 6	3 − 3 = 0

Hence, the correct option is: c) 3 and 3

1 The sum of two numbers is 18 and difference is 0. Guess the two numbers.

    a)   9 and 8   b)   9 and 9   c)   10 and 9   d)   8 and 8

2 The sum of two numbers is 14 and the difference is 2. Guess the two numbers.

a) 7 and 7   b) 9 and 5   c) 12 and 2   d) 8 and 6

3 The sum of two numbers is 24 and the difference is 8. Guess the two numbers.

a) 16 and 8   b) 18 and 10   c) 14 and 10   d) 20 and 4

4 The difference of two numbers is 6 and their sum is 8. Guess the two numbers.

a) 9 and 1   b) 7 and 1   c) 10 and 2   d) 6 and 2

5 The difference of two numbers is 1 and their sum is 11. Guess the two numbers.

a) 5 and 4   b) 7 and 6   c) 6 and 5   d) 8 and 3

6 The difference of two numbers is 3 and their sum is 15. Guess the two numbers.

a) 9 and 6   b) 9 and 5   c) 8 and 8   d) 8 and 6

7 The sum of two numbers is 14 and the difference is 6. Guess the two numbers.

a) 12 and 2   b) 10 and 4   c) 11 and 4   d) 10 and 5

8 The sum of two numbers is 25 and the difference is 15. Guess the two numbers.

a) 15 and 10   b) 24 and 1   c) 21 and 4   d) 20 and 5

9 The sum of two numbers is 50 and the difference is also 50. Guess the two numbers.

a) 50 and 50   b) 25 and 25   c) 50 and 0   d) 30 and 20

10 The difference of two numbers is 30 and their sum is 90. Guess the two numbers.

a) 60 and 30   b) 50 and 40   c) 45 and 45   d) 90 and 0

2   Code Messages

	1	2	3	4	5	6	7	8	9	10	11	12	13
Letter	A	B	C	D	E	F	G	H	I	J	K	L	M
Code	+	=	x	%	&	^	*	$	#	@	!	{	]

	14	15	16	17	18	19	20	21	22	23	24	25	26
Letter	N	O	P	Q	R	S	T	U	V	W	X	Y	Z
Code	<	/	;	,	}	.	>	-	[	|	:	?	\

Example: Code the word BEAUTIFUL

a)   =&+_>#^_{

b)   =&_>^@#}

c)   %&(^#@!+

d)   =&x:?#^_{

Answer: On coding the word beautiful we get =&+_>#^_{ . Hence, the answer is: a) =&+_>#^_{

1 Code the word CLOCK

a)   xxxxx   b)   x{/x!   c)   x)x;/   d)   x?xx!

2 Code the word CHOCOLATE

a)   ^%$@#&.,% b)   x&*(/{+>& c)   x$/x^*></ d)   x$/x/{+>&

3 Code the word SPOON

a) .;\\>   b) ,;\/>   c) .;//<   d) *\/<

4 Code the word APPLE

a)   +//{&   b)   +;;{&   c)   <';{&   d)   &$${&

7

5 Code the word FRIEND

    a) **)&<%   b) ^^*&<%   c) ^}#&<%   d))(*%$%

6 Code the word GIRAFFE

    a) *&}+^^&   b) ^%|+^^&   c) &()^*^&   d) *#}+^^&

7 Code the word TABLE

    a) >+={&   b) ++>{&   c) >+=}$ d) >|l\&

8 Code the word SCHOOL

    a) .x&V{   b) .x$//{   c) .#&V{   d) ,+$//{

9 Code the word MEDICAL

    a) {*$#x+{   b)]$&*x+{   c)]?%#.<{   d)]&%#x+{

10 Code the word ELEPHANT

    a) ${$;$+<>   b) ${$;&+<>   c) &{&;$+<>   d) #{#;&+<>

Q2. **Using the same table of codes as above, decode the following messages in the blank space below:**

Example: .$+{{ |& %+<x&

Answer: On decoding the message .$+{{ |& %+<x& we get, shall we dance. Hence, the answer is: Shall we dance

1 # {#!& |#<>&}.

___ ____ _____

3 # {/[& %/*.

___ ____ _____

2 =& x+}&^_{

___ ____

4 >$#<! ;/.#>#[&

____ ____

5 .$& #. .{&&;#<*

___ ___ ___

6 }&+% >$& <&l.;+;&}

___ ___ ___

7 x{/.& >$& =//!

___ ___ ___

8 ;+x! ?/_} =+*

___ ___ ___

9 ;#x! _; >$& =/>>{&

___ ___ ___ ___

10 &+> ?/_} {_<x$

___ ___ ___

3   Ranking

Example: A pile has 15 notebooks. Ronny's notebook is 7th from the top. What is the position of Ronny's notebook from the bottom of the pile?

a) 8th

b) 9th

c) 10th

d) 11th

Answer: The position of Ronny's notebook from the bottom of the pile is 9th.

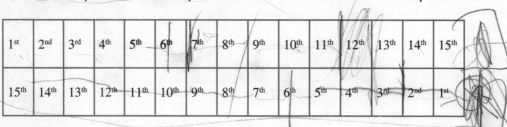

1st	2nd	3rd	4th	5th	6th	7th	8th	9th	10th	11th	12th	13th	14th	15th
15th	14th	13th	12th	11th	10th	9th	8th	7th	6th	5th	4th	3rd	2nd	1st

Hence, the answer is: b) 9th

1   25 people are standing in a row at a form collection centre. Jack is 19th from the counter. Three people ahead of Jack walk away without depositing their form. Find the position of Jack.

    a)   11th   b)   13th   c)   15th   d)   16th

2   What is the position of Jack from the end?

    a)   12th   b)   10th   c)   7th   d)   5th

3 A photograph shows 11 men standing in a row. Mr John is at the centre. What is his position from the left?

    a)   6th   b)   5th   c)   7th   d)   4th

4 What is Mr John's position from the right?

    a)   4th   b)   5th   c)   6th   d)   7th

5 13 girls are standing in a line. Betty is standing 4th from the left. Find her position from the right.

    a)   10th   b)   11th   c)   9th   d)   8th

6 A pile has 32 notebooks. Den's notebook is 12th from the top. What is the position of her book from the bottom?

    a)   19th   b)   20th   c)   22nd   d)   21st

7 If the topmost and the bottommost notebooks are removed, what will be the position of Den's notebook from the top of the pile?

    a)   9th   b)   10th   c)   11th   d)   12th

8 If the topmost and the bottommost notebooks are removed, what will be the position of Den's notebook from the bottom of the pile?

    a)   19th   b)   20th   c)   21st   d)   22nd

9 A file has 28 test papers numbered 1 to 28. Tom's test paper is numbered 15th. What is its position from the end?

    a)   11th   b)   12th   c)   13th   d)   14th

10 If the first five test papers are removed, find the position of Tom's test paper from the end.

    a)   14th   b)   13th   c)   12th   d)   11th

Q2. Ten friends go to see a movie. Unfortunately, they get different seats in different rows. There are 15 seats in each row. In total, there are 12 rows in the hall. The first row is marked as A and the last row is marked as L. When looked at from the front, George's seat is C 10. Read the clues given below and answer the following questions:

Example: Daniel's seat is 2 rows behind George's. What is Daniel's seat 's number?

a) F 10

b) E 10

c) F 12

d) E 12

Answer: Since Daniel is sitting exactly 2 seats behind George's, Daniel's seat number is: b) E 10.

1. Alana's seat is 5 seats to the left of George's. Find the seat number of Alana.

   a) C 5 b) C 6 c) C 4 d) C 3

2. Ronny's seat is 2 seats to the right of George's. Find the seat number of Ronny.

   a) C 10 b) C 11 c) C 12 d) C 13

3. Abel's seat is 3 seats to the left of Ronny's but one row behind it. Find the seat number of Abel.

   a) B 8 b) B 9 c) D 8 d) D 9

4. Frank's seat is the last seat in row A. Find the seat number of Frank.

   a) A 14 b) A 15 c) A 12 d) A 13

5 Mathew's seat is 7 seats to the left of Abel's. Find the seat number of Mathew.

a) D 1   b) D 2   c) D 3   d) D 4

6 Mark's seat number is the same as Mathew's but two rows in front of Mathew's. Find the seat number of Mark.

a) B 2   b) B 3   c) B 4   d) B 5

7 Peter's seat is four places to the right of Matthew's. However, he is not in the same row as Matthew's but placed five rows behind. Find the seat number of Peter.

a) I 2   b) J 2   c) I 6   d) J 6

8 Paul and Peter share the same seat number. However, Paul is placed one row behind Peter's. What is the seat number of Paul?

a) I 3   b) I 2   c) J 5   d) J 6

9 Sam's seat is the first seat in row F. What is his seat number?

a) F 1   b) F 2   c) D 1   d) D 2

10 Victor's seat is 7 seats to the right of Sam's. What is the seat number of Victor?

a) F 7   b) F 8   c) F 9   d) F 10

4 Mirror Images

Example:

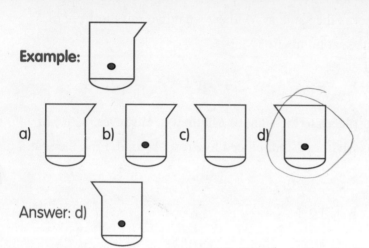

a)   b)   c)   d)

Answer: d)

1

a)   b)   c)   d)

2
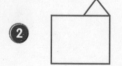

a)   b)    c)   d)

3

a) 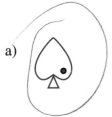　　b) 　　c) 　　d)

4

a) 　　b) 　　c) 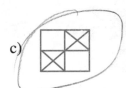　　d)

5

a) 　　b) 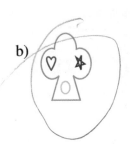　　c) 　　d)

6

a) 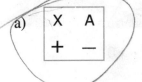　　b) | + | A |
X	−	c)	A	X
+	−	d)	−	A
+	X

7

a) b) c) d)

8

a) b) c) d)

9

a) b) c) d)

10

a) b) c) d)

16

Choose the correct mirror image of the following numbers:

Example: 11

a) 1-1   b) 1-1   c) 1-1   d) 11

Answer: b) 1-1

① 4

a) 4   b) 4   c) 4   d) 4

② 5

a) 5   b) 2   c) 5   d) 5

3 33

a)  ƐƐ b)  ƷƐ c)  (ƐƷ) d)  ƐƷ

4 7

a)  ⊥ b)  ⊥ c)  ⊥ d)  (7)

5 69

a)  99 b)  66 c)  (69) d)  99

6 42

a)  24 b)  (42) c)  24 d)  42

7 81

a) 18 (circled)   b) 18   c) 18   d) 18

8 56

a) 56 (circled)   b) 56   c) 65   d) 95

9 99

a) 99   b) 96   c) 99   d) 99 (circled)

10 73

a) 73 (circled)   b) 73   c) 73   d) 73

5 Classification

Out of the codes given in each problem, four are similar in a certain way. Find the code which is different from the rest.

Example:
a) A10
b) B20
c) C30
d) D40
e) E55

Answer: Except code e, all other codes have multiples of 10. Therefore, the different code is:

1
a) 113   b) 223   c) 334
d) 445   e) 556

2
a) A1B   b) B2C   c) C3D
d) D7E   e) E5F

3
a) DEF   b) GHI   c) JKM
d) MNO   e) PQR

4
a) Z45   b) Y40   c) X35
d) W30   e) V22

5
a) L12   b) M13   c) N11
d) O15   e) P16

20

6
a) 111H
b) 222I
c) 333J
d) 445K
e) 555L

7
a) 1a26z
b) 4d17q
c) 12m19t
d) 5e24x
e) 19s20t

8
a) DE7
b) EF11
c) FG21
d) GH28
e) HI35

9
a) 101P
b) 102Q
c) 103Z
d) 104S
e) 105T

10
a) Z26
b) Y27
c) X24
d) W23
e) V22

Q2. Out of the given items, one is different from the others. Find out the different or the odd item from the following options:

Example:
a) Tie
b) Car
c) Gloves
d) Belt
e) Socks

Answer: Except option (b), all the other items are accessories. Car is a vehicle, therefore the odd item is: b) Car

1
a) Chips
b) Knife
c) Burger
d) Pizza
e) Sandwich

2
a) China   b) Africa   c) Asia
d) Australia   e) Europe

3
a) May   b) April   c) Saturday
d) March   e) June

4
a) Floppy   b) CD   c) ipod
d) Pen drive   e) Hard disk

5
a) Bat   b) Dolphin   c) Camel
d) Polar Bear   e) Snake

6
a) Television   b) Fan   c) Clock
d) Refrigerator   e) Bulb

7
a) Cup   b) Saucer   c) Teapot
d) Breadstick   e) Spoon

8
a) New York   b) California   c) London
d) Chicago   e) Los Angeles

9
a) Dog   b) Pen   c) Tree
d) Man   e) Lizard

10
a) Water   b) Pool   c) River
d) Pond   e) Lake

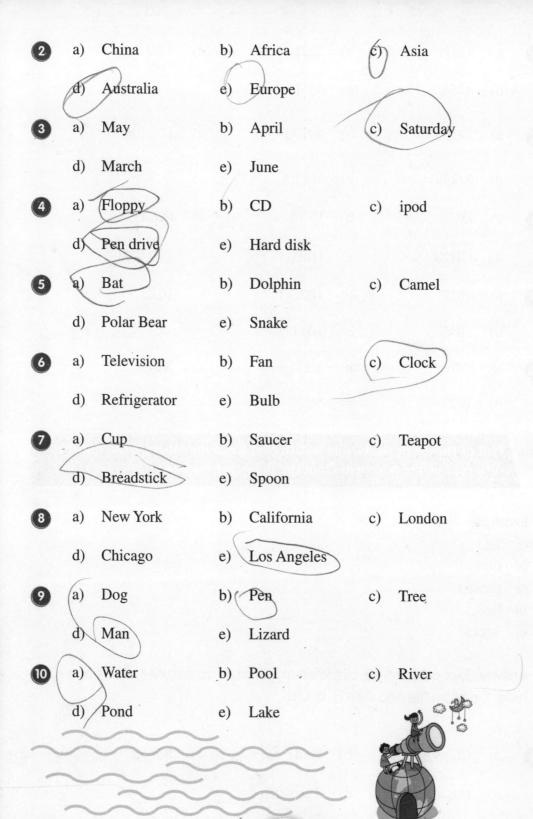

22

6 Figure Series

Example:

a)   (b)   c)   d)

Answer: Since a similar figure is being repeated at every alternate step in the given series, the correct option is:

b)

1

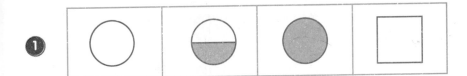

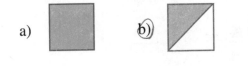   

a)   b)   c)   d)

2

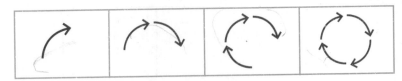

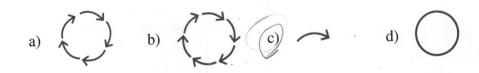

a)   b)   c)   d)

23

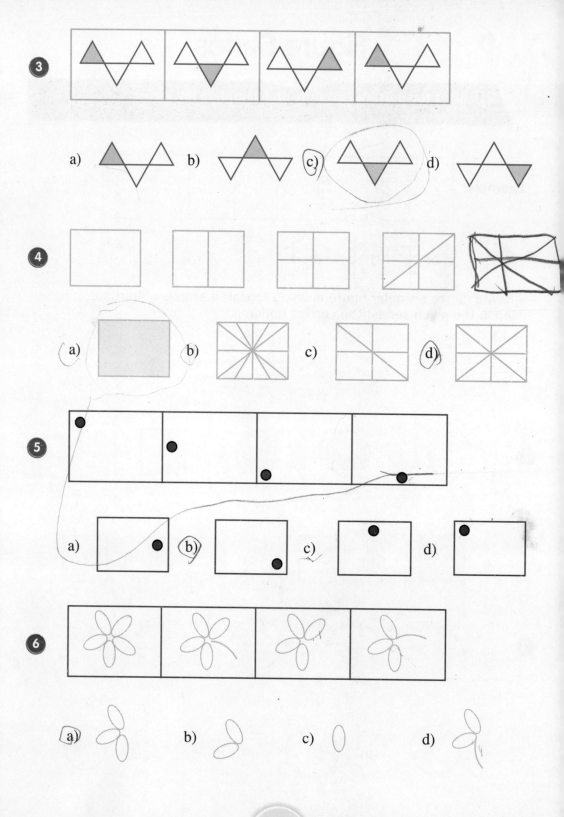

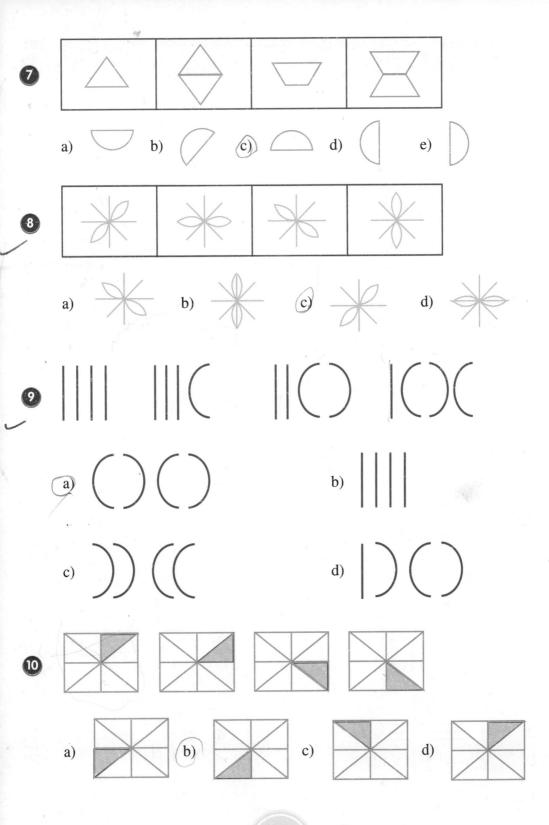

7

a)   b)   c)   d)   e)

8

a)   b)   c)   d)

9

a)   b)

c)   d)

10

a)   b)   c)   d)

Example:

a)    b) 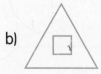   c)    d)

Answer: In every step of the series, the small inner figure becomes the large outer figure and a new small figure is introduced, which again in the next step becomes the large outer figure. Therefore, the correct answer is:

a)

 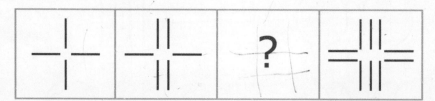

a) 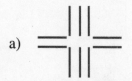   b)

c)   d)

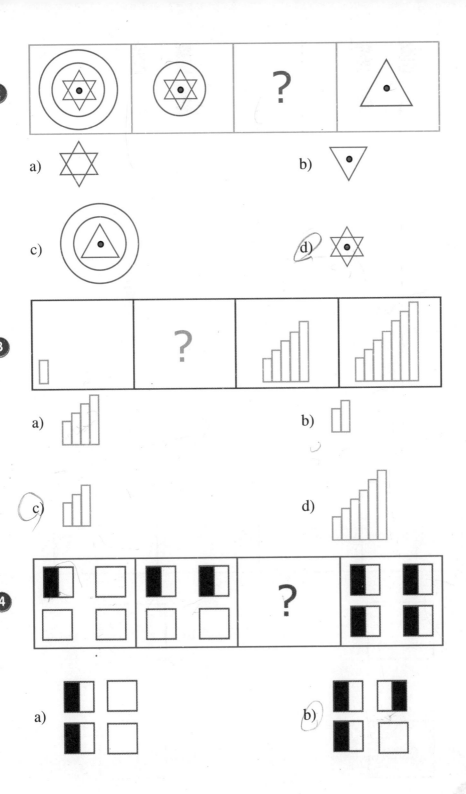

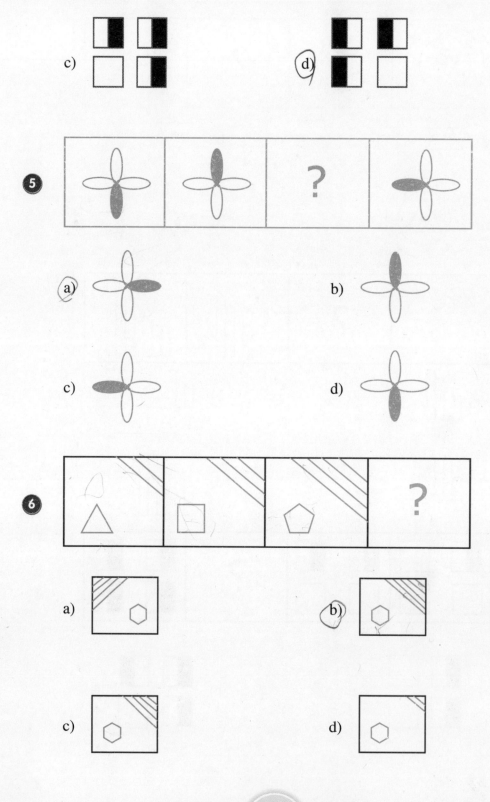

c)

d)

5

a)

b)

c)

d)

6

a)

b)

c)

d)

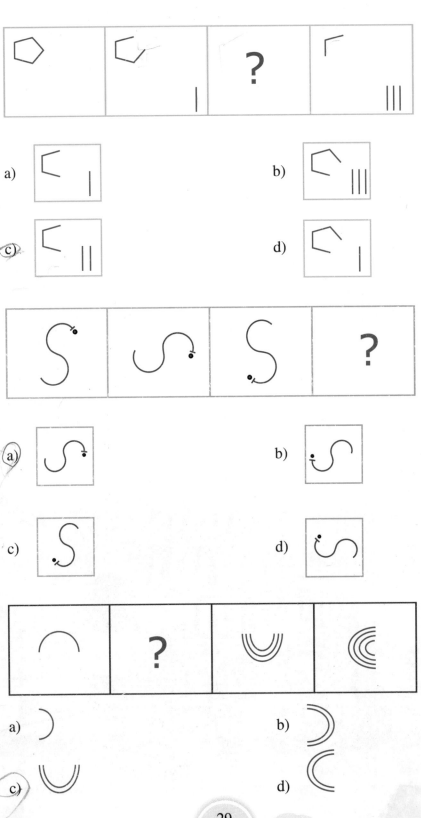

7

a)

b)

c)

d)

8

a)

b)

c)

d)

9

a)

b)

c)

d)

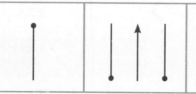

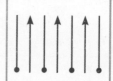

a)

b)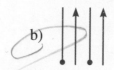

c)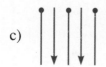

d)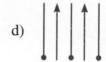

Sequencing

Example: How many times is 😊 followed by 😧?

😊😑😧😊☠😊😑😊😧☠😧😑☹☠😊😑😧☠😊😧

a) 1
b) 2
c) 3
d) 4

Answer: The sequence shows that 😊 is followed by 😧 only twice.
Therefore, the correct answer is: b) 2

1 How many times is ☠ is followed by 😊?

😊😑😧😊☠😊😑😊😧☠😧😑☹☠😊😑😧☠😑😧

a) 1   b) 3   c) 2   d) 5   e) 6

2 How many times does the hand point out only one finger?

a) 4   b) 5   c) 6   d) 7

3 How many times is the letter box open?

a) 4   b) 5   c) 6   d) 7

4 How many times is an open letter box followed by a closed letter box?

a) 4   b) 3   c) 5   d) 2

31

5 How many times is a three-sided figure preceded by a four-sided figure?

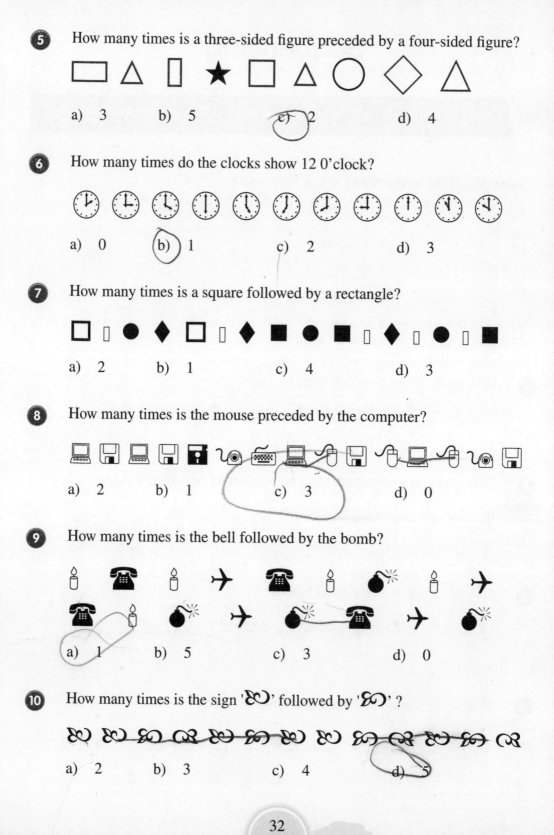

   a) 3   b) 5   c) 2   d) 4

6 How many times do the clocks show 12 0'clock?

   a) 0   b) 1   c) 2   d) 3

7 How many times is a square followed by a rectangle?

   a) 2   b) 1   c) 4   d) 3

8 How many times is the mouse preceded by the computer?

   a) 2   b) 1   c) 3   d) 0

9 How many times is the bell followed by the bomb?

   a) 1   b) 5   c) 3   d) 0

10 How many times is the sign 'ಜಾ' followed by 'ಜಾ' ?

   a) 2   b) 3   c) 4   d) 5

Q2. Arrange the following objects according to the increasing order of their size and tick the correct option:

Example: elephant, rabbit, rat, kangaroo

a) rabbit, rat, elephant, kangaroo
b) rat, rabbit, elephant, kangaroo
c) elephant, rabbit, rat, kangaroo
d) rat, rabbit, kangaroo, elephant

Answer: On arranging the mammals according to their sizes, the sequence will be as follows: rat, rabbit, kangaroo, elephant. Therefore, the correct option is: d) rat, rabbit, kangaroo, elephant.

1 segment, line, point, ray

a) point, segment, line, ray   b) point, segment, ray, line

c) ray, line, segment, point   d) line, ray, segment, point

2 room, country, building, city

a) room, building, city, country   b) city, room, building, country

c) building, country, room, city   d) country, building, room, city

3 minute, day, fortnight, year

a) minute, day, fortnight, year   b) minute, fortnight, day, year

c) day, minute, year, fortnight   d) day, year, minute, fortnight

4 eraser, pencil box, bag, book

a) pencil box, bag, book, eraser   b) bag, pencil box, book, eraser

c) eraser, book, pencil box, bag   d) eraser, pencil box, book, bag

5 refrigerator, television, mobile phone, pen drive

a) pen drive, mobile phone, television, refrigerator

b) television, mobile phone, refrigerator, pen drive

c) pen drive, mobile phone, refrigerator, television,

d) pen drive, refrigerator, television, mobile phone

8 Puzzles

Example: There are three friends. One likes to eat chocolate, the second one likes to eat cakes and the third one likes to eat pizza. Boya does not eat pizza or cake, and the one who eats cake is also not Tim. The third friend is Anna.

i) Who eats cakes?
   a) Boya
   b) Anna
   c) Tim

ii) Who eats pizza?
   a) Boya
   b) Anna
   c) Tim

iii) Who eats chocolates?
   a) Boya
   b) Anna
   c) Tim

Answer:

	Pizza	Cake	Chocolate
Boya	✗	✗	✓
Tim	✓	✗	✗
Anna	✗	✓	✗

Therefore, Boya eats chocolates, Tim eats pizza and Anna eats cakes.
Hence, the answers are:
i) c. Anna
ii) b. Tim
iii) c. Boya

1 There are five friends and each has a pet. The pets are: dog, cat, rat, fish and parrot. A and B do not like cats and dogs. B and C do not like fishes and parrots. C and D do not like cats and rats. D and E do not like fishes.

i) Who has the dog?

   a) B   b) C   c) A   d) D

ii) Who has the fish?

   a) E   b) C   c) A   d) B

iii) Who has the cat?

   a) B   b) C   c) D   d) E

iv) Who has the parrot?

   a) C   b) E   c) D   d) A

v) Who has the rat?

    a) A   b) B   c) C   d) D

2

A. Five friends are sitting around a round table in a restaurant. P is sitting next to Q, R is sitting between Q and S and T is sitting to the left of P.

i) Who is sitting to the left of S?

    a) T   b) R   c) P   d) Q

ii) Who is sitting to the right of P?

    a) R   b) S   c) Q   d) T

iii) Who is sitting to the right of R?

    a) S   b) P   c) Q   d) T

iv) Who is sitting to the left of Q?

    a) R   b) P   c) S   d) T

v) Who is sitting between P and S?

    a) T   b) R   c) P   d) Q

vi) Who is sitting between R and P?

    a) T   b) R   c) P   d) Q

vii) Who is sitting between T and R?

    a) R   b) P   c) S   d) Q

viii) Who is sitting between Q and S?

    a) R   b) S   c) P   d) T

B. Now if A and B join the table such that A sits between T and P, whereas B sits between Q and R. Then, answer the following:

i) Who is sitting to the left of A?

    a) T   b) P   c) B   d) Q

ii) Who is sitting to the right of B?

    a) P   b) Q   c) R   d) T

iii)   Who is sitting to the left of P?

    a) T   b) Q   c) B   d) A

iv) Who is sitting between B and S?

    a) T   b) R   c) A   d) Q

3   Five students from section A, B, C, D and E each are selected for a debate competition. Tom and Jack are not in section B, C or D. David and Jim are not in A or B. Tom and David are not in section C or E. The fifth friend is Betty.

i)   Who is in section A?

    a) Jack   b) David   c) Tom   d) Betty

ii)   Who is in section C?

    a) Jack   b) David   c) Jim   d) Betty

iii) Who is in section E?

    a) Jack   b) David   c) Tom   d) Betty

iv) Who is in section B?

    a) Jack   b) Jim   c) Tom   d) Betty

v)   Who is in section D?

    a) Jim   b) David   c) Jack   d) Betty

4   A family of three people has 3 cars. The father and the son do not drive the black car. The mother and the son do not drive the white car.

i)   Who drives the white car?

    a) Father   b) Mother   c) Son

ii)   Who drives the red car?

    a) Mother   b) Father   c) Son

iii) Who drives the black car?

    a) Son   b) Father   c) Mother

9 Time

Q1. **Look carefully at the clock and answer the questions that follow:**

Example:

What time will it be after three hours and twenty-five minutes have passed?
a) 8:30
b) 8:35
c) 9:30
d) 9:35
Answer: 5:05 + 3 hours and 25 mins = 8:30
Therefore, the correct option is: a) 8:30

①

i)   What time will it be after one hour and forty-five minutes have passed?

a) 7:10   b) 6:10   c) 6:15   d) 5:15

ii)   What time will it be after three hours and twenty-minutes have passed?

a) 7:35   b) 7:30   c) 7:45   d) 7:40

iii) What time will it be after five hours and five minutes have passed?

    a)   9:30   b)   9:25   c)   9:40   d)   9:35

iv) What time will it be after eight hours and fifty minutes have passed?

    a)   1:15   b)   2:10   c)   1:30   d)   2:35

v) What time will it be after two hours and thirty minutes have passed?

    a)   6:50   b)   6:45   c)   6:40   d)   6:55

2

i) What time will it be after one hour and five minutes have passed?

    a)   12:40   b)   12:45   c)   12:50   d)   12:55

ii) What time will it be after four hours and twenty-five minutes have passed?

    a)   4:05   b)   4:10   c)   4:00   d)   4:10

iii) What time will it be after ten hours and ten minutes have passed?

    a)   8:50   b)   8:40   c)   9:40   d)   9:50

iv) What time will it be after six hours and twenty minutes have passed?

    a)   6:10   b)   6:00   c)   5:00   d)   5:10

v) What time will it be after three hours and forty-five minutes have passed?

    a)   3:20   b)   3:10   c)   3:25   d)   3:15

Q2. **Look at the calendar of March 2012 and answer the questions that follow:**

Example:

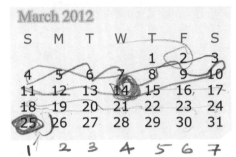

March 2012

S	M	T	W	T	F	S
				1	2	3
4	5	6	7	8	9	10
11	12	13	14	15	16	17
18	19	20	21	22	23	24
25	26	27	28	29	30	31

APR. 1 2 3 4 5 6 7

If today is 9 March 2012, what date was it 2 days ago?

a) 8th

b) 7th

c) 6th

d) 5th

Answer: Two days ago, the date was 7th March 2011. Therefore, the correct option is: b) 7th

1 If today is 25 March 2012, what date was it 7 days ago?

a) 20th   b) 21st   c) 18th   d) 19th

2 If today is 2 March 2012, what date will it be 10 days from now?

a) 16th   b) 12th   c) 11th   d) 15th

3 If today is 14 March 2012, what date will it be 8 days from now?

a) 22nd   b) 21st   c) 23rd   d) 20th

4 What will be the date on the second Sunday of the month?

a) 9th   b) 10th   c) 12th   d) 11th

5 What will be the date on the fourth Monday of the month?

a) 25th   b) 26th   c) 24th   d) 23rd

Look at the calendar of August and answer the questions that follow:

Example:

August						
S	M	T	W	T	F	S
			1	2	3	4
5	6	7	8	9	10	11
12	13	14	15	16	17	18
19	20	21	22	23	24	25
26	27	28	29	30	31	

If today is 21 August, then what date was it 11 days ago?
a) 8th
b) 9th
c) 10th
d) 5th

Answer: 11 days ago, the date was c) 10th

1. What will be the date on the third Friday of the month?

   a) 17th   b) 18th   c) 19th   d) 20th

2. What will be the date on the first Tuesday of the month?

   a) 2nd   b) 3rd   c) 6th   d) 7th

3. If today is 18 August, what date was it 6 days ago?

   a) 10th   b) 9th   c) 12th   d) 11th

4. If today is 22 August, what date will it be 4 days from now?

   a) 25th   b) 26th   c) 24th   d) 27th

5. What will be the date on the last Thursday of the month?

   a) 29th   b) 31st   c) 28th   d) 30th

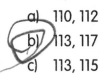

10

Missing Numbers

Example: 101, 103, 107, 109, ___, ___

a) 110, 112

b) 113, 117

c) 113, 115

d) 117, 120

Answer: The numbers in the series above are prime numbers, therefore the correct option is: b) 113, 117

1   32, 40, 48, 56, ___, ___

   a)   64, 72   b)   62, 70   c)   61, 71,   d)   68, 78

2   7, 21, 35, 49, ___,

   a)   56, 63   b)   63, 77   c)   63, 70   d)   56, 70

3   100, 80, 60, 40, 20, ___

   a)   20, 10   b)   30, 20   c)   20, 0   d)   30, 0

4   18, 38, 58, 78, ___, ___

   a)   98, 118   b)   98, 108   c)   88, 98   d)   88, 108

5   234, 345, 456, 567, ___, ___

   a)   567, 678   b)   678, 698   c)   678, 789   d)   678, 8910

Q2. Study the pattern in fig. A and fill the missing number in fig. B:

Example:

a) 9   b) 10   c) 11   d) 12

Answer: The pattern is 7 + 9 – 4 = 12. Therefore, 11 + 5 – 7 = 10

1

a)   11   b)   12   c)   13   d) 14

2

a) 0   b)   1   c)   2   d)   3

3

a)   15   b)   24   c) 12   d)   10

42

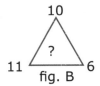

a) 9   b) 15   c) 13   d) 17

 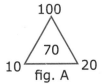 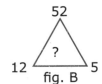

a) 35   b) 30   c) 50   d) 45

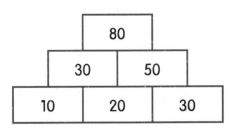 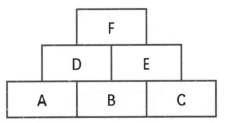

Example:

	90		
	20	70	
?	?	60	

a) 10, 20   b) 10, 10   c) 5, 10   d) 5, 5

Answer: The pattern is A + B = D, B + C = E and D + E = F
Therefore, the correct answer is 10 + 10 = 20. Hence, the correct option is:
b) 10, 10

1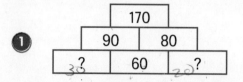

a) 30, 40   b) 30, 30   c) 30, 20   d) 20, 20

2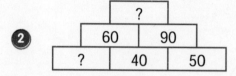

a) 20, 150   b) 20, 180   c) 30, 150   d) 30, 200

3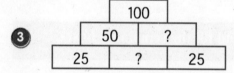

a) 30, 40   b) 30, 50   c) 25, 50   d) 25, 40

4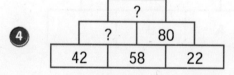

a) 110, 180   b) 100, 180   c) 110,190   d) 100, 190

5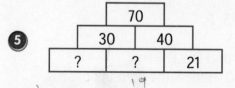

a) 11, 20   b) 10, 20   c) 10, 19   d) 11, 19

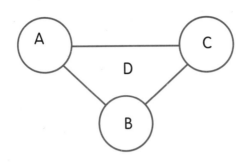

Where A x B x C = D

Example:

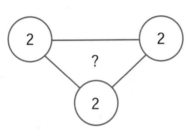

a) 6   b) 10   c) 8   d) 4

Answer: Since the pattern is A x B x C = D, therefore 2 x 2 x 2 = 8.
Hence, the correct option is: c) 8

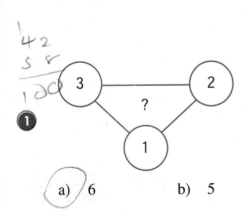

a) 6   b) 5   c) 4   d) 7

45

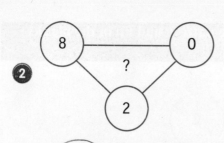

2

a) 6 b) 0 c) 18 d) 4

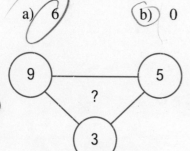

3

a) 135 b) 100 c) 115 d) 125

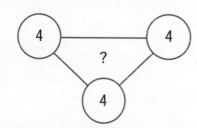

4

a) 8 b) 16 c) 12 d) 64

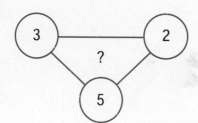

5

a) 10 b) 30 c) 15 d) 20

Answers

1. Guessing Number

Q1.

1. d	2. c	3. a	4. b	5. a
6. c	7. d	8. d	9. b	10. a

Q2.

1. b	2. d	3. a	4. b	5. c
6. a	7. b	8. d	9. c	10. a

2. Code Messages

Q1.

1. b	2. d	3. c	4. b	5. c
6. d	7. a	8. b	9. d	10. c

Q2.

1. I like winters
2. Be careful
3. I love dogs
4. Think positive
5. She is sleeping
6. Read the newspaper
7. Close the book
8. Pack your bag
9. Pick up the bottle
10. Eat your lunch

3. Ranking

Q1.

1. d	2. b	3. a	4. c	5. a
6. d	7. c	8. b	9. d	10. a

Q2.

1. a	2. c	3. d	4. b	5. b
6. a	7. c	8. d	9. a	10. b

4. Mirror Images

Q1.

1. d	2. b	3. a	4. c	5. b
6. a	7. b	8. d	9. a	10. b

Q2.

1. b	2. a	3. c	4. d	5. c
6. b	7. a	8. b	9. d	10. a

5. Classification

Q1.

1. a	2. d	3. c	4. e	5. c
6. d	7. c	8. b	9. c	10. b

Q2.

1. b	2. a	3. c	4. c	5. e
6. c	7. d	8. c	9. b	10. a

6. Figure Series

Q1.

| 1. b | 2. a | 3. c | 4. d | 5. b |
| 6. a | 7. c | 8. c | 9. a | 10. b |

Q2.

| 1. b | 2. d | 3. c | 4. d | 5. a |
| 6. b | 7. c | 8. d | 9. b | 10. c |

7. Sequencing

Q1.

| 1. b | 2. c | 3. d | 4. a | 5. a |
| 6. b | 7. d | 8. a | 9. d | 10. c |

Q2.

| 1. b | 2. a | 3. a | 4. d | 5. a |

8. Puzzles

Q1.

1. i) b   ii) c   iii) d   iv) c
   v) b
2. A)
   i) b   ii) c   iii) a   iv) b
   v) a   vi) d   vii) c   viii) a
   B)
   i) a   ii) c   iii) d   iv) b
3. i) c   ii) c   iii) a   iv) d

v) b

4. i) a   ii) c   iii) c

9. Time

Q1.

1. i) b   ii) c   iii) a
   iv) a   v) d
2. i) b   ii) a   iii) d
   iv) b   v) c

Q2.

| 1. c | 2. b | 3. a | 4. d | 5. b |

Q3.

| 1. a | 2. d | 3. c | 4. b | 5. d |

10. Missing Numbers

Q1.

| 1. a | 2. b | 3. c | 4. a | 5. c |

Q2.

| 1. d | 2. a | 3. c | 4. b | 5. a |

Q3.

| 1. c | 2. a | 3. c | 4. b | 5. d |

Q4.

| 1. a | 2. b | 3. a | 4. d | 5. b |